D1552810

Good & Noble Heart
10-Week Transformation

JOHN BRADBURY

Copyright © 2019 John Bradbury

All rights reserved.

ISBN: 9781695855038

All Scripture quotations are from the
New King James Version (NKJV)
© Thomas Nelson 1982

*To all of you who want nothing more than to put a smile on Jesus' face--
this book is for you.*

*May you learn the difference between trying to ACT like His disciple
through the force of your will and BECOMING His disciple with
identity-based transformation.*

*First, change the way you think. Next, love yourself well. And finally,
bear much fruit. That is your mission should you choose to accept it,
as they say. May this book be a tool that propels you in that direction.*

How to use this book...

"If I will change, everything will change for me."
-- Jim Rhon

"But the ones that fell on the good ground are those who, having heard the word with a noble and good heart, keep it and bear fruit with patience." -- Jesus, Luke 8:15

You were born to **bear fruit**, to produce results that add value to your life, others, and the world around you. That is how you glorify God.

To do so, you must change your IDENTITY, or **the way you think about yourself**. This book is designed to help you do that. It will not do it for you, but it is a powerful TOOL you can use to speed up the process.

As long as you think like an ORPHAN, feel like a VICTIM, and act as if you live in a world of SCARCITY, **you can't bear fruit.**

The GOOD & NOBLE HEART 10-WEEK TRANSFORMATION walks you through the New Testament in four chapters a day, challenging you to think about yourself as God does. It also provides you with a daily guided journal assignment to help you PRACTICE what you are learning.

I plead with you to take this transformation seriously. The best way to use this book is to LISTEN to the assigned chapters, READ the devotion, and WRITE in the guided journal each day. Combine it with other habits like a walk outside and healthy food choices, and you have the recipe for a morning, lunch-time, or evening routine that will change your life.

Take the time to MEDITATE as often as you can. Sit still without distractions, or go on a jog or walk so you can WATCH YOURSELF THINK. This practice will help you detach your true identity from your thoughts, feelings, and actions, enabling you to cultivate a fertile heart the way a gardener tends her garden.

When you discover how God thinks about you, PRACTICE thinking about yourself the same way. Talk to yourself the way the Father speaks to you, and allow His opinion to shape your identity.

TAKE RESPONSIBILITY for every thought, emotion, and action in your life. There are many things you don't control-- the weather, other people, the government, God, the enemy, your past, etc.-- practice humility and accept what you can't change. But NEVER ALLOW YOURSELF TO BECOME A VICTIM! **What goes on inside of you is what determines if you bear fruit, and you have full control of that.**

You are the gardener, and your life is the garden-- love yourself well. Your circumstances (past or present) do not need to change. YOU NEED TO CHANGE.

This is your opportunity to transform your life and never go back-- SEIZE IT! In about thirty minutes a day for ten weeks, you can think about yourself in a new way, which will change everything.

The world needs you at your best. Go for it.

John Bradbury

Good & Noble Heart
10-Week Transformation

LISTEN to four chapters a day,
starting in Matthew.

READ the corresponding devotion
and let it change the way you think.

WRITE the guided journal assignment
to engage with what you're learning.

ALLOW God's thoughts about you
to shape your identity.

PRACTICE thinking of yourself
the same way.

DAY 1: Matthew 1-4

Making The Transition

And suddenly a voice came from heaven, saying, "This is My beloved Son, in whom I am well pleased."

For years you've lived a normal life, but something is shifting inside you.

It's like a grand old clock is chiming in your soul, declaring that it's time. Time for what, you're not sure, but SOMETHING is happening.

You want more. Your restless heart searches for answers, and before long, you arrive at a place of decision.

With no assurances about what's next, you head down to the river of surrender.

Before God and everyone, you decide to GO ALL IN, giving yourself wholly to the King and His kingdom.

You long for intimacy, influence, impact, and increase, so you ready yourself to take the plunge.

You dive in, surrendering everything to the will of God, then emerge to the bright light of revelation.

"You are my beloved Son, in whom I am well pleased," rings in your ears, a vote of confidence from the Father.

The Spirit of God comes upon you, empowering you for the task ahead.

Normal is over-- time to change the world.

Today is the day you make the commitment to Love Yourself Well. What can you do today to agree with the Father and live like His beloved son?

_____

_____

_____

_____

_____

_____

_____

_____

_____

_____

_____

_____

_____

_____

_____

_____

_____

_____

_____

DAY 2: Matthew 5-8

If You Are The Son Of God

Now when the tempter came to Him, he said, "If You are the Son of God..."

IF. **All the enemy needs to derail your future is one IF.**

Certain things ONLY exist because God said so; you can't prove them.

God forgave you. The Father accepted you, adopting you into His family and providing you with significance, identity, and purpose. The Holy Spirit anointed you and called you to change the world. **You can't do those things for yourself, neither can you prove that they are real.**

The WORDS OF GOD create the core beliefs that lay the foundation for your future success; there is no other evidence. Therefore, for you to become who God made you to be, you MUST start with FAITH in what He says about you.

God will speak to you-- through the Bible, impressions, dreams, prophecies, sermons, teachings, songs, unusual circumstances, visions, etc...-- and then you must believe Him. Don't look around your life or heart for proof that He is right. **God's words create reality; they do not require proof.**

You believe what God says about you with CERTAINTY, and live as if everything He says is accurate in the present moment.

You can't "work on" becoming a son, receiving a calling, feeling forgiven-- those things are only valid because God said so.

You either BELIEVE it and begin thinking, talking, and acting like it's already true, or Satan will bully you into a life of survival in the wilderness.

What IF question is creating doubt and holding you back, and what has God said that you can PRACTICE believing to overcome it?

_____

_____

_____

_____

_____

_____

_____

_____

_____

_____

_____

_____

_____

_____

_____

_____

_____

_____

_____

_____

DAY 3: Matthew 9-12

Moved With Compassion

But when He saw the multitudes, He was moved with compassion for them, because they were weary and scattered, like sheep having no shepherd.

The foundation of all lasting change is compassion. Think about that statement for a moment, then consider all the other techniques we use to motivate ourselves. We tend to bully through fear or manipulate with the promise of reward, and those work for a while, but the motivation wanes with time, and we end up back where we started.

Instead of trying to force change, try leading yourself with genuine compassion. Take the time to acknowledge the real and immediate problems you face. Don't sugar coat them-- let reality set in. ACCEPT THE WAY THINGS ARE. Then allow yourself to feel genuine compassion for yourself, asking, "How did I end up here?" and "What do I need to change?"

We all need inspiration, belief, examples, instruction, leadership, accountability, resources, and community to create new habits. **Without compassion, we look for excuses for our failure instead of setting ourselves to succeed.**

Compassion says that your heart is good, your problems are real, and you can do it with the right help. It pushes us to seek the Lord for solutions and to implement the answers we get in prayer.

Quit bullying yourself long enough to assess your situation. Have you been struggling in the same areas for months or years? **Stop the cycle of manipulation that leads to half-hearted action that produces shame and eventually makes you quit. Let compassion move you.**

Humility is accepting the way things are. Compassion is giving yourself everything you need to succeed without bullying. How can you demonstrate humility and self-compassion today?

_____

_____

_____

_____

_____

_____

_____

_____

_____

_____

_____

_____

_____

_____

_____

_____

_____

_____

_____

_____

_____

DAY 4: Matthew 13-16

Becoming Good Soil

But others fell on good ground and yielded a crop: some a hundredfold, some sixty, some thirty.

If you get this concept, you get everything, so listen up.

God is the initiator of all good things. He SPEAKS to us IDEAS from heaven, each of which contains the potential to change the world. Everything He says is packed with wisdom and grace and is ready to grow and bear fruit.

BUT MOST OF WHAT GOD SAYS DOES NOT BEAR FRUIT.

His words wither, not because the ideas are bad or the circumstances are wrong; **they wilt because of the condition of the heart that receives them.** You must understand and accept responsibility for your mind, emotions, and desires before anything will change in your life.

For your heart to be GOOD SOIL that grows God's ideas and produces loving relationships, influence, miracles, and resources, you must believe the following:

I am a world changer! I have a unique identity and purpose that is critical to the building of the kingdom, and I can hear from God. My life is my responsibility, my heart is GOOD, and I am no longer a victim or an orphan!

It's my job to cultivate confidence, motivation, and wholeness-- my happiness is up to me. I am not waiting on God, and the enemy will not steal from me. **I am supposed to live a life of abundance!**

*Good ideas are EASY-- it's **practice and implementation** that hold us back. The condition of your heart-- your confidence level, willingness to take responsibility, and abundance mindset-- changes everything. How can you develop the soil of your heart today?*

_____

_____

_____

_____

_____

_____

_____

_____

_____

_____

_____

_____

_____

_____

_____

_____

_____

_____

DAY 5: Matthew 17-20

Nothing Is Impossible

If you have faith as a mustard seed, you will say to this mountain, 'Move from here to there,' and it will move; and nothing will be impossible for you.

Ever faced an impossible situation? How did you feel?

If you are like the disciples in Matthew 17, you felt helpless and frustrated. They faced a difficult and emotional problem, and they tried their best to solve it, but nothing worked. Jesus came and cleaned up their mess, but rebuked them in the process. Later, they got Jesus alone and asked Him what they did wrong. "Why could you solve the problem, and we got stuck?"

"Because of your unbelief," He said, and went on to explain the problem in more detail. Do you remember how I taught you to cultivate your heart into good soil so you can receive my words and grow them? Well, you're doing an excellent job hearing my words and producing fruit in your own life, but when you get into a situation where you are the sower, you freeze up. **You know how to receive from God, but you don't understand how to be Jesus in the story.**

If you have faith as a mustard seed, Jesus went on to explain, then you can speak to impossibilities, and they will move. The mustard seed is tiny, but it sprouts immediately and grows into the largest of all the herbs. **You need to switch gears, with the help of some prayer and fasting, from receiver to sower.**

You must believe that you can speak to problems and release powerful solutions. If you think like that, the way I do, **nothing will be impossible** for you.

If you're feeling overwhelmed by an impossible situation, perhaps a change in perspective is in order. What would your life look like if you were Jesus in the story instead of the one who needs to be rescued?

_____

_____

_____

_____

_____

_____

_____

_____

_____

_____

_____

_____

_____

_____

_____

_____

_____

_____

_____

_____

DAY 6: Matthew 21-24

Greatness

Whoever desires to become great among you, let him be your servant.

The orphan mentality longs to win the lottery.

We wish for the big promotion or raise that does not carry any extra responsibility.

We daydream of the handsome and wealthy husband riding in to rescuing us.

We imagine what we would do if we invested a few dollars, and it magically turned into millions.

We wonder what it would be like to be born into a wealthy family or to grow up with natural beauty, athletic ability, or a genius IQ.

We call this wishful thinking HOPE.

Oh God, let me keep thinking, feeling, and acting the same way but get better results!

I want a great marriage, family, career, business, bank account, impact, or whatever, but I want You to give it to me.

But the kingdom doesn't work that way.

Jesus loves His people to desire greatness, but it doesn't come through the divine lottery system. **Greatness is reserved for those who serve the most people at the deepest level.**

You were born for GREATNESS. Who can you serve, and what problem can you solve, to walk worthy of the calling on your life?

_____

_____

_____

_____

_____

_____

_____

_____

_____

_____

_____

_____

_____

_____

_____

_____

_____

_____

_____

_____

_____

_____

DAY 7: Matthew 25-28

Survival Sucks

For to everyone who has, more will be given, and he will have abundance; but from him who does not have, even what he has will be taken away.

"You wicked and lazy servant." Ouch-- I don't want to hear that from Jesus. What did the guy in the parable do to deserve such harsh criticism?

He survived. He paid his bills, maintained his house, and showed up for his job. He took the identity, revelation, gifts, anointing, opportunities, and relationships he received and kept them safe. From the outside, he looked faithful, but on the inside, fear ruled his heart.

"I didn't know what to pursue, so I played it safe," he said, but Jesus could not believe His ears. "I didn't come from heaven, turn the world upside down, sacrifice my life, rise from the dead, and pour out My Spirit so you could play it safe!"

If you follow the King, you live in a kingdom. You rule and conquer, and you INCREASE what you receive from heaven. **If you are a disciple of the World Changer, you must become a world changer**-- there are no believers who hide in fear.

Lift your vision higher! Learn to take your five talents and turn them into ten-- and refuse to settle for "faithful."

If you are not increasing your influence, love, miracles, and resources, it's time to re-evaluate.

Enough hiding in fear, holding on until the Lord comes.

Let's change the world.

What talents are you being "faithful" with instead of multiplying? How can you change that?

DAY 8: Mark 1-4

Follow Me!

He went up on the mountain and called to Him those He Himself wanted. And they came to Him.

Jesus wants to talk to you for a minute: "Will you meet with me for a second, I have something I want to ask you? I have a plan. **I'm taking over the world, and I want you to help me.**

I am building a kingdom, and my agenda is to empower every person on the planet. **I want to eradicate poverty, disease, anxiety, depression, racism, violence, fear, addiction, and divorce-- will you help me?**

My vision is an earth covered with worship, revelation, inspiration, and the anointing of My Spirit, where every person has a loving family, health and fitness, nutritious food, safety, identity and purpose, and meaningful work.

I need you to **stop worrying about all the stuff others fret about and GO ALL IN.** If you believe me, I'll give you everything you need to succeed. I'll provide forgiveness, acceptance, community, inspiration, revelation, grace, authority, anointing, gifts-- anything you need, it's yours. And I'll be right there with you every step of the way.

Let's make a deal. You stop worrying about the things you need to survive and let me take care of that. Instead, fellowship with my Spirit every day, asking, '**How can we take over the world today?**'

Let go of your insecurities and fears, and say yes to starting businesses, going on camera, leading organizations, creating products, loving the unlovable, training the next generation, and solving problems. **Are you in?**"

Are you ALL IN? How can you serve Jesus' agenda to transform the world?

_____

_____

_____

_____

_____

_____

_____

_____

_____

_____

_____

_____

_____

_____

_____

_____

_____

_____

_____

_____

_____

_____

_____

DAY 9: Mark 5-8

Accept The Word

These are the ones sown on good ground, those who hear the word, accept it, and bear fruit.

I know you heard from God; He said something about WHO YOU ARE that got you excited. Think about it-- the One whose words created everything spoke to you too. **Then why aren't you changing the world right now?**

Here are three possible reasons:

1. When God spoke to you, you heard what He said through the lens of insecurity, discounted it, and the enemy stole the word from you.
2. When you listened to what He said, you got excited and began to pursue it, but the unresolved pain from your past stunted its growth. Grief, unforgiveness, betrayal, fear, depression, or anger caused your enthusiasm to wane, and what God said withered under the heat of those overwhelming emotions.
3. When God spoke to you, His word immediately started to prosper inside you, but financial pressure, busyness, and stress siphoned your focus away.

Let's be honest. You're not waiting on God, fighting the devil, or suffering oppression from others. **If we're not growing God's ideas into loving relationships, increased influence, abundant resources, and miracles, it's because we're scared, hurt, or stressed out.** BUT THAT CAN CHANGE RIGHT NOW!

The condition of your heart doesn't change because you "work on it" for a long time. **It changes by BELIEVING what God says about you, ACCEPTING it, and LIVING as if it is already true.**

If you BELIEVE what God has already told you, how would your life change?

_____

_____

_____

_____

_____

_____

_____

_____

_____

_____

_____

_____

_____

_____

_____

_____

_____

_____

_____

_____

DAY 10: Mark 9-12

What's The Problem?

I have compassion on the multitude, because they have now continued with Me three days and have nothing to eat.

Jesus is the ultimate problem solver-- He'll tackle anything, no matter how big or small. When you follow Him, it's only a matter of time until He recruits you to help. So my question is, **what problem is Jesus asking you to help solve?** In Psalm 72 you see Jesus' vision for the planet. His agenda includes:

Salvation-- He desires every person to feel forgiven, clean, and whole.
Adoption-- He wants us to reconnect with the Father, and to understand our unique identity and purpose.
Empowering-- He longs to fill people with His Spirit, giving them access to revelation, power, and love.
Freedom-- Jesus wants to deliver every person from depression, anxiety, addiction, and torment.
Health-- He desires all to live whole physically, mentally, and emotionally.
Nutrition-- He wants everyone to have enough nutritious food and clean water.
Safety-- He desires a world without war or violence.
Justice-- He longs to build communities without prejudice, racism, oppression, or fear.
Righteousness-- Jesus is the King of doing things the right way.
Excellence-- He knows how to do education, government, and business.
Abundance-- He wants each person to do meaningful work and have more than enough resources.
Family-- He desires to eradicate loneliness and promote genuine love.
Worship-- Jesus is all about honoring the Father with the extravagant worship He deserves.

What problem do you feel Jesus' compassion about, and how can you help Him solve it?

_____

_____

_____

_____

_____

_____

_____

_____

_____

_____

_____

_____

_____

_____

_____

_____

_____

_____

_____

DAY 11: Mark 13-16

What Now?

Peter called to mind the word that Jesus had said to him, "Before the rooster crows twice, you will deny Me three times." And when he thought about it, he wept.

You just blew it big time. The thing you thought you would never do-- even promised to do the opposite-- you did. God trusted you with an assignment, and you let Him down. You were supposed to be the leader, the person others could count on, and **now you're blubbering with your head buried in your hands.** WHAT NOW?

What do you do when fear overwhelms your faith, and you do the opposite of what you wanted to? **You cry.**

The worst thing you can do in those moments is to pick yourself up and move on-- you need to grieve. It's not about giving in to shame or having a pity party; **it's about being honest with yourself.** Before you can recover and grow into the person you need to be, you MUST tell yourself the truth, and allow the tears to flow.

If you don't grieve your mistakes and failures, admitting the cold, hard facts, you can't move on. **If you make up a story to temporarily cheer yourself up, you'll trap those emotions and regrets inside to resurface later.**

THE FOUNDATION OF ALL HAPPINESS AND WHOLENESS IS HUMILITY-- ACCEPTING THE WAY THINGS ARE.

Jesus can restore, disciple, and empower you for the assignment ahead if you cry when you make a mistake. Don't let busyness keep you from grieving, repentance, and being honest with yourself.

What do you need to be HONEST about to yourself and God? How can you GRIEVE so that you can move forward?

_____

_____

_____

_____

_____

_____

_____

_____

_____

_____

_____

_____

_____

_____

_____

_____

_____

_____

_____

_____

_____

_____

DAY 12: Luke 1-4

Greatness Is Going First

"He will also go before Him in the spirit and power of Elijah, 'to turn the hearts of the fathers to the children,' and the disobedient to the wisdom of the just, to make ready a people prepared for the Lord."

Do you ever feel like you're always the first one out of all your friends and family to do stuff?

Maybe you're the first one to finish college, start a business, write a book, record an album, or lose weight.

Perhaps the message God called you to trumpet is something no one around you has heard before. Being the pioneer clearing the land can feel lonely, but you are not alone.

I understand how you feel.

MOST OF THE TIME BEING GREAT MEANS GOING FIRST.

Please don't make the mistake I did for many years. I was willing to go before others, but I didn't gather and lead them all the way to the finish line.

If you are the forerunner in your sphere of influence, remember, you are not alone. God is raising up people like you all over the earth.

Say yes to selling, gathering, leadership, and organizing. **Don't show others what to do and then leave them to figure it out for themselves-- guide them all the way to success.**

Are you tired of always being first, feeling lonely because no one understands you? How can you accept the mantle of leadership, create community, and help others get the results they need?

_____

_____

_____

_____

_____

_____

_____

_____

_____

_____

_____

_____

_____

_____

_____

_____

_____

_____

_____

_____

_____

DAY 13: Luke 5-8

I'm The One

And He began to say to them, "Today this Scripture is fulfilled in your hearing."

At some point, God will call your name, asking you to help solve a problem. If you believe Him and respond, the Father will anoint you with His Spirit, empowering you with the revelation and power you need to do the task.

Then it's time for the test. The enemy and your circumstances will scream the exact opposite of what God said about you, to see if you believe God's words just because He spoke them.

When you pass the test, you will walk out of survival and begin doing what you are called to do. People will respond, and you'll use the anointing on your life to help solve problems.

Then something strange will happen. You'll be excited about what you're learning and the results you're getting, but **the people that knew you while you were still a survivor will be skeptical.** Many of them will not be able to get over the fact that you grew up with them or used to be in the same place they are now.

What are you going to do? Are you going to tone it down, back off, and fit in with your friends and family? **Nope.** You are going to stand up and say, **"I am the answer to your prayers and the one you've been waiting for-- God anointed me to solve the problem you are struggling with."** Most of them won't respond, but things will shift inside you.

You are no longer the survivor they remember; **you are the anointed of the Lord.**

The people that know you well often have a hard time receiving from the anointing on your life. How are you going to guard your heart from offense and continue to grow into who you are called to be?

DAY 14: Luke 9-12

How You Hear

"Therefore take heed how you hear. For whoever has, to him more will be given; and whoever does not have, even what he seems to have will be taken from him."

"I need to hear from God," we say. Whenever there is a crisis to avert, a problem to solve, a decision to make, or a fear to overcome, we long for God to speak to us. We know that if God talks, somehow things will work out, and we're right. The voice of God is the most potent force in the universe, initiating every good thing.

We value what God says and how He says it, tuning our ears to the impression, sermon, song, dream, prophecy, or unusual coincidence that we hope will guide us. **But we often ignore how we hear.** I don't mean the way we hear from God-- **I am referring to the perspective through which we filter His words.**

You see, everything God says, even the slightest impression, has the potential to grow into a fruitful idea that changes the world. However, it is not what **God says that matters most; it is the condition of the listener's heart that counts.** The way we think determines the fruitfulness of our lives.

We often make negative assumptions like the world is getting worse, Christianity is on the decline, I am just not good at that, my heart is deceitful, I can't trust my desires, someone else is to blame, I can't control how I feel, I don't have the time, money, or energy, and I don't know how. The list could go on and on, but you get the point.

When we look at the world, others, and ourselves through a lens of fear and doubt, THE IDEAS GOD GIVES US DON'T GROW. For things to change in your life, THE WAY YOU THINK MUST CHANGE FIRST.

God will talk to you if you will listen, but that doesn't guarantee success.
What are you currently doing to improve the condition of your heart
(soil) so that God's words prosper inside of you?

_____

_____

_____

_____

_____

_____

_____

_____

_____

_____

_____

_____

_____

_____

_____

_____

_____

_____

_____

_____

DAY 15: Luke 13-16

Your Level Of Service

When an innumerable multitude of people had gathered together, so that they trampled one another...

How much personal development do you need to survive? **None.**

If you don't see yourself as the kind of person who serves others, you won't even try to cultivate a good and noble heart.

YOUR LEVEL OF PERSONAL DEVELOPMENT CORRELATES DIRECTLY TO THE LEVEL YOU BELIEVE YOU ARE CALLED TO SERVE OTHERS.

If you're only going to feed yourself, why start farming?

You won't-- you'll go to the store and buy only the food you need.

If you want to feed a family all year round, you cultivate a garden. An acre of ground is plenty to provide for even the largest of families.

But if you believe you are called to serve thousands, then you MUST develop yourself on a larger scale.

Your ability to communicate, lead, forgive, sell, delegate, learn, think, focus, and control your emotions must flourish if you desire to serve the masses.

If you want to grow, focus on your IDENTITY. Find out what God wants you to do and who He called you to serve, then dedicate your imagination, belief, focus, and desire to SERVING at your maximum capacity.

Dream BIGGER. What level of service will REQUIRE you to develop yourself as a person?

_____

_____

_____

_____

_____

_____

_____

_____

_____

_____

_____

_____

_____

_____

_____

_____

_____

_____

_____

_____

_____

DAY 16: Luke 17-20

Becoming Profitable

"So likewise you, when you have done all those things which you are commanded, say, 'We are unprofitable servants. We have done what was our duty to do.' "

Getting into the Kingdom of Heaven is free. Well, not exactly-- it's the most expensive thing ever, costing Jesus His life-- **but it costs you nothing.** All you have to do is humble yourself, admit that Jesus is the only way, and BELIEVE.

Believe that the Father created all things, and He wants you as His own. Believe that Jesus died for you, rose again, and ascended into heaven, preparing the way for you to connect with the Father.

Believe that the Spirit of God dwells inside you, empowering you with revelation, grace, and the anointing. Believe that every word God speaks about you is true, and receive those words with confidence, wholeness, and focus.

So, you're in God's kingdom, now what? You got in for free, but God made a BIG investment to adopt you and empower you to change the world-- and **He expects a return on His investment.**

God is not running a charity-- He desires those who have freely received to give back, making the world a better place.

He expects you to believe every word He says, no exceptions. He requires you to take the gifts He gave and steward them well. He demands obedience when He tells you to do something-- every time.

God wants you to long for more, to become addicted to the anointing and maximize your influence to help others.

Are you doing only what is required of you? Less? More? How can you become profitable in the kingdom?

_____

_____

_____

_____

_____

_____

_____

_____

_____

_____

_____

_____

_____

_____

_____

_____

_____

_____

_____

_____

_____

DAY 17: Luke 21-24

Your Life Matters

I bestow upon you a kingdom, just as My Father bestowed one upon Me.

As the Father gave Jesus an assignment and the authority to fulfill it, Jesus is calling you.

You don't need to worry about the resources necessary to do your job-- God will take care of that. **Your job is to get clear answers to some vital questions.**

Who am I called by God to serve? What problems am I supposed to solve? What sphere of influence am I called to bless? How do I access the anointing and resources God made available for me to do my job? Am I willing to become a servant leader, an example for others to gather around? Will I persevere through opposition and give my life to fulfill God's plan?

If you get crystal clear about your IDENTITY, or WHO GOD CALLED YOU TO BE, then confidence, motivation, happiness, and focus will follow.

You are called to lead, sell, serve, solve problems, and add value-- we all are-- and God will reward you for your service.

Jesus is a King, ruling a Kingdom, with the expressed purpose of taking over the world. But the way He leads separates Him from every other King. Jesus gets down in the dirt with His people, empowering them to make a meaningful contribution to the world around them.

Now He is calling you to do the same.

Who will remain stuck if you do not reach your full potential? What are you going to do about that?

_____

_____

_____

_____

_____

_____

_____

_____

_____

_____

_____

_____

_____

_____

_____

_____

_____

_____

_____

_____

_____

DAY 18: John 1-4

Come And See

They said to Him, "Rabbi" (which is to say, when translated, Teacher), "where are You staying?" He said to them, "Come and see."

How do you take a bunch of average guys and turn them into world changers? First of all, let's get one thing straight-- **ordinary people are the only kind of people there are.** If you think successful people were born with something special that you don't have, your dead wrong. No one is inherently better than anyone else.

So how do you turn regular folks into world changers? It starts with a basic understanding of how God created us. When the Father designed humans, **He hard-wired us to live by faith.** God talks, revealing the incredible story of why we're here, how to prosper, and what the future holds, and we BELIEVE what He says.

When we see where we fit in the story, that forms our IDENTITY, which is the foundation of all we do. So, to answer the original question-- **you turn ordinary people into world changers by SELLING them on their place in the story**, our redemption through Jesus, and the advancing Kingdom of God. When we IDENTIFY where we fit in the story, our confidence, motivation, happiness, and focus develop, and we are ready to learn HOW.

Notice how Jesus called the disciples. He didn't teach them how to have a better marriage or convince them to show up at the synagogue more often. He SOLD them, with John's help, on the fact that He was the Messiah, the One initiating the Kingdom of God. Then He SOLD them on where they fit in the story. **Before they ever heard a word of teaching, they were ALL IN, eager to listen to everything Jesus said.**

Do you know the bigger story and where you fit in it? What can you PRACTICE thinking about yourself today to reinforce your identity?

_____

_____

_____

_____

_____

_____

_____

_____

_____

_____

_____

_____

_____

_____

_____

_____

_____

_____

_____

_____

DAY 19: John 5-8

Kingdom Logic

You search the Scriptures, for in them you think you have eternal life; and these are they which testify of Me.

If you follow Jesus as your Lord and Savior, you have to believe His teachings. If you receive Jesus' words as truth, you must understand that you are adopted, forgiven, accepted, and empowered by the Spirit of God.

If you know that you are a child of God, then it stands to reason that you are a king and a priest with access to heaven and authority over the enemy. Therefore, **if you are a believer in Jesus, you are a WORLD CHANGER**-- it is impossible to hear His words and remain an orphan or a victim.

But I feel like a victim! I'm barely surviving out here, struggling with my health, relationships, finances, and inner life-- how can you say I am a world changer? Let me share an incredible truth with you (it could be the most valuable thing you've ever heard!) **Are you ready?**

IDENTITY + INTIMACY = IMPACT

Get a clear understanding of your identity (where you fit in the story, what Jesus did for you, and who you are called to be.) Add regular time with Jesus loving Him and paying attention to what He says.

And you will start to bear fruit. Your impact (the love, miracles, influence, and resources you produce) will increase and add value to the people around you.

Then you can multiply that impact by learning how to sell, lead, and cooperate with the Holy Spirit. **Ready to change the world?**

The sign that you're still identifying as a victim is BLAME. Is there any area of your life that you're blaming others for your lack of progress?

_____

_____

_____

_____

_____

_____

_____

_____

_____

_____

_____

_____

_____

_____

_____

_____

_____

_____

_____

_____

_____

_____

DAY 20: John 9-12

Confident Humility

"I am the light of the world. He who follows Me shall not walk in darkness, but have the light of life."

Jesus looked at them straight in the eyes and said, **"I am the light of the world."** In other words, "I am the answer to your problems. Follow me, and you will end up in the right place."

However, Jesus gladly admitted that without the Father's blessing and assistance, He could do nothing.

That is the position you find yourself in today.

Jesus commissioned you, declaring that you are the light of the world. He also said that as the Father sent Him, He is sending you.

You are Jesus in the story.

Can you look someone in the eyes and tell them to follow you into health, forgiveness, happiness, peace, love, and abundance?

Do you think, feel, and act like the light of the world? **If not, you need to grow your confidence.**

At the same time, you must never forget Who your source is. Without the revelation, love, acceptance, grace, mercy, and power you receive from heaven, you have nothing to offer.

You must walk in BOTH extreme confidence and humility. People are waiting for you to shine bright so they can follow you into the light.

Humility is NOT a lack of confidence or shying away from the spotlight. What are you going to do today to increase your confidence?

_____

_____

_____

_____

_____

_____

_____

_____

_____

_____

_____

_____

_____

_____

_____

_____

_____

_____

_____

_____

DAY 21: John 13-16

Assume God Is With You

I am the vine, you are the branches. He who abides in Me, and I in him, bears much fruit; for without Me you can do nothing.

"Without Me, you can do nothing." I've heard that statement Jesus told His disciples in John 15 most of my life, leading me to believe I was missing some "special" relationship with God that only the "anointed" people possessed.

But that's not what Jesus meant. He was illustrating to His disciples THE MODEL we are to follow-- the relationship He had with the Father.

Jesus taught them that **you need two things to bear fruit: identity and intimacy.**

You must BELIEVE that God is GOOD, you are GOOD, and the purpose for which God created you is GOOD. Then you live aware of God's presence by talking to Him, listening to Him, and loving Him.

With those things in place, you will bear fruit-- it is that simple.

If you want to bear more fruit, you either **improve your identity** (think about yourself better), or **increase your intimacy** (live more aware of His presence), or both.

It is true that without Him you can do nothing, but that is not the point-- Jesus is pulling back the curtain and revealing how to bear fruit through abiding in His love.

ALWAYS ASSUME THAT JESUS IS WITH YOU, and you will produce genuine love, abundant resources, miracles, and increasing influence.

What can you PRACTICE today that will improve your IDENTITY and increase your INTIMACY with God?

_____

_____

_____

_____

_____

_____

_____

_____

_____

_____

_____

_____

_____

_____

_____

_____

_____

_____

_____

_____

DAY 22: John 17-20

Father, Glorify Your Son

Father, the hour has come. Glorify Your Son, that Your Son also may glorify You.

Father, make me famous.

Set me up as an example for many people to follow.

Glorify me.

Let light, hope, and revelation stream from me to the world around, guiding them to you.

I am your Son, and I want to be just like you.

Make me famous, an example, a leader, and a voice for my generation.

Look no farther-- let Your favor, love, and power rest on me, and use me however you desire.

You said I am the light of the world, and I believe you.

Don't hide me any longer.

I refuse to allow insecurity and fear to restrict Your anointing on my life.

Speak to me, and I will joyfully receive Your words and grow them with confidence.

Enough of the small stuff-- let's do something **BIG** together.

Can you pray a prayer like Jesus prayed in John 17 ABOUT YOURSELF with faith in your heart? Why or Why Not?

_____

_____

_____

_____

_____

_____

_____

_____

_____

_____

_____

_____

_____

_____

_____

_____

_____

_____

_____

_____

_____

_____

DAY 23: John 21 - Acts 3

I Also Send You

So Jesus said to them again, "Peace to you! As the Father has sent Me, I also send you."

"As the Father sent Me, I also send you." Let that statement resonate through your heart and mind for a minute.

The Father chose Jesus before the foundation of the world to change the course of history and redeem humanity. He sent Jesus with ALL the authority of Heaven to gather a group of people to Himself, demonstrate the heart of the Father, and teach them about the Kingdom.

The Father asked Jesus to draw huge crowds, become a public figure, offer a new opportunity, give His life for His people, and empower them to pick up where He left off.

"As the Father sent Me..." You are sent with the same authority and agenda, to bring Heaven to earth and change the course of history. **"I also send you..."**

YOU ARE NOT ON THIS PLANET TO SURVIVE! You are a voice, a leader, and a perfect reflection of the One who sent you.

BELIEVE what I am saying to you right now and GO ALL IN. When you BUY INTO the calling on your life, your mind, heart, mouth, and actions will follow.

QUIT looking for evidence God's words about you are accurate-- **let His voice create the reality INSIDE you**, and it will eventually manifest to the world.

How BIG are you willing to think? If everyone believed about themselves what you believe about yourself, would the planet get better or worse?

_____

_____

_____

_____

_____

_____

_____

_____

_____

_____

_____

_____

_____

_____

_____

_____

_____

_____

_____

_____

_____

DAY 24: Acts 4-7

Boldness

Now when they saw the boldness of Peter and John, and perceived that they were uneducated and untrained men, they marveled. And they realized that they had been with Jesus.

How many ideas have you had in the last year?

How many encounters with God have you experienced?

Remember feeling His presence in worship or any light bulb moments while studying the Scriptures?

Did you have any dreams, desires, and impressions that you believe were inspired by God?

You know the difference between those who are changing the world and those who are not?

The first group thinks of themselves as world changers-- they consider every idea, dream, desire, or encounter to be a seed they can grow into something awesome. **They are able to change the way they think, feel, and talk based on what God says, and they take immediate ACTION to turn His words into results.** Because they BELIEVE a whisper from God can change history and BUY INTO their identity as a world changer, they have BOLDNESS to act.

"God, give me MORE BOLDNESS! Give me the confidence to speak, sell, lead, recruit, create, and pray crazy big prayers!"

Change the way you think about yourself, and you will change the world.

Good ideas do not change the world-- God ideas that grow and mature in a GOOD heart do. What ACTION can you take today to ensure that the words you hear from God are not wasted?

_____

_____

_____

_____

_____

_____

_____

_____

_____

_____

_____

_____

_____

_____

_____

_____

_____

_____

_____

DAY 25: Acts 8-11

Doubting Nothing

While Peter thought about the vision, the Spirit said to him, "Behold, three men are seeking you. "Arise therefore, go down and go with them, doubting nothing; for I have sent them."

What is the difference between you and Peter? He was a regular guy with a typical job, trying to do the best he could for his family-- and then he met Jesus.

Jesus was fascinating and mysterious, and **Peter left behind survival in pursuit of impact.** In one day everything changed-- but Peter was still Peter.

With his big mouth and limited patience, Peter experienced some incredible moments (he walked on water!), and some disappointing setbacks (he rebuked and denied Jesus.)

Then he quit. He decided he was not good enough to be what Jesus wanted him to be, so he went back to survival. Jesus, however, can be very persuasive. He restored Peter, recommissioned him, and empowered him with the Holy Spirit.

Fast forward a few years... Peter is sitting on a roof praying and worshiping. The Holy Spirit shows him a vision, instructing him to go against everything he was taught growing up. Then he hears from God-- the same Holy Spirit who talks to us gives him an impression just like he does right now. **"Get up and act, doubting nothing."** So Peter, going way outside his comfort zone, took action.

GET UP AND ACT, DOUBTING NOTHING!

Has doubt stolen your ability to take action? How can you use Peter's story to remember WHO YOU ARE? What PRACTICE can you do today to move forward with something God put on your heart?

_____

_____

_____

_____

_____

_____

_____

_____

_____

_____

_____

_____

_____

_____

_____

_____

_____

_____

_____

_____

DAY 26: Acts 12-15

Sent By The Spirit

The Holy Spirit said, "Now separate to Me Barnabas and Saul for the work to which I have called them."

About one out of a hundred believers end up on staff at a church, non-profit, or missions organization. **But what about the rest of us? What are we supposed to do with our lives?**

The checklist for a typical believer not "called to the ministry" looks something like this:

Go to church as often as possible. Give money to the church (bonus points for giving 10%!) Be nice. Tell a few people a year about Jesus, or invite them to church. Spend the other 95% of your week in survival mode trying to pay bills, deal with problems, and take care of your family.

I don't know about you, but that sounds boring. I think every believer is "called" to advance the Kingdom of God, whether they are on staff at a church or not, and I think we should all do it for a living. **There should be no survivors, victims, or orphans among us.**

The agenda of King should be the agenda of every person in the Kingdom: Connect every person on earth with the Father. Improve physical, mental, and emotional health. Destroy the work of the enemy, including addiction, divorce, and torment. Keep people free and safe. Grow and distribute an abundance of nutritious food. Create wealth and solve problems. Care for and train the next generation. Cover the earth with worship and revelation. Increase beauty and joy in the world.

What are you being sent by the Spirit to do?

How can you align your life with Jesus' mission to make the earth look like heaven?

_____

_____

_____

_____

_____

_____

_____

_____

_____

_____

_____

_____

_____

_____

_____

_____

_____

_____

_____

_____

_____

DAY 27: Acts 16-19

Changing The World

These who have turned the world upside down have come here too.

Am I crazy?

Why am I so driven to make an impact, do something meaningful, and change the world?

I look around and wonder-- what does it feel like to be normal? Everyone else is dropping their kids off at school, going to work, and heading home. Maybe they want more, but I'm not sure.

There is something inside me that screams for greatness, and it scares me.

What's wrong with me? I feel irresponsible. I feel embarrassed.

The craving to learn and grow consumes me, and when I can't figure something out, it's difficult to sleep.

I love my family, and I want to provide security for them, but it's hard to focus on survival.

I know I'm almost there, just one idea away from a breakthrough.

My biggest fear is that the world will be the same with or without me, that I won't make a difference.

I was born to turn the world upside down-- I know it.

I just know it.

Are you driven to make the world a better place? How can you throw fuel on that fire?

_____

_____

_____

_____

_____

_____

_____

_____

_____

_____

_____

_____

_____

_____

_____

_____

_____

_____

_____

_____

_____

_____

Baptized In Fire

He said to them, "Did you receive the Holy Spirit when you believed?"

"Into what then were you baptized?" Paul asked. **That's a good question.**

To be baptized into something is to STOP identifying yourself one way, and START identifying yourself another. **It's all about BUY-IN.**

A leader stands up and shouts, "Follow me to get these results!" and you BELIEVE what they say and IDENTIFY as their disciple. Baptism is the public demonstration that you're ALL IN.

John baptized people into repentance, preparing their hearts and minds for Jesus. When you BELIEVED what John said, you demonstrated it by getting dunked in the river.

After you identify yourself as humble, repentant, and ready for a new life, the natural progression is to believe in Jesus. He is the way you connect with the Father and start over as a child of God.

But things don't stop there. When you BELIEVE what Jesus says, you demonstrate it by IMMERSION in the Spirit of God.

There is no other alternative-- **to be Jesus' disciple is to do the things Jesus does with the tools that Jesus uses.**

Go ALL IN. Don't settle for humility and repentance; move on to revelation, power, love, faith, and the anointing.

Let Jesus baptize you in the Holy Spirit and FIRE.

How long has it been since you were immersed in the Holy Spirit?
What practices can you put in place to ensure regular encounters with
His power?

_____

_____

_____

_____

_____

_____

_____

_____

_____

_____

_____

_____

_____

_____

_____

_____

_____

_____

_____

DAY 29: Acts 24-27

Waiting For A Sign?

I saw a light from heaven, brighter than the sun, shining around me and those who journeyed with me.

What are you called to do? "I'm not called to do anything. I've never been knocked off my horse by a light from heaven!" **Really?** Do you know how many people saw a light brighter than the sun and heard an audible voice to get them to pursue God's purpose for their life? **One.**

But every believer is a son or daughter-- we are ALL kings and priests to our God. We each have a unique identity and purpose that helps build the kingdom. There is no such thing as "secular" work or "just paying the bills" if you're a disciple of Jesus. **If you're waiting for a light from heaven to force you to turn around, then you are headed the wrong way!**

The usual way you find out what you're called to do is much more subtle. Sure, you'll have some encounters with God along the way, but you don't need to wait for them-- **go after them!**

Everyone starts in the same place. You humble yourself and repent, trusting Jesus to save you. Then you find someone you know is called by God, follow them, and immerse yourself in the things of the kingdom.

Paying attention to every dream, desire, impression, prophecy, and testimony, you follow the voice of God refusing to let fear hold you back. **Always assume that God has something BIG for you to do, and be willing to SERVE your way to the top.**

Treasure each encounter you have with the Lord, subtle or loud, and take action to fulfill God's call on your life.

Are you waiting for some dramatic sign to propel you into advancing the kingdom? What subtle clues has God already given you that you may be ignoring, i.e. inspiration stories, desires, or good examples?

_____

_____

_____

_____

_____

_____

_____

_____

_____

_____

_____

_____

_____

_____

_____

_____

_____

_____

_____

_____

DAY 30: Acts 28 - Romans 3

Glory, Honor, & Immortality

Eternal life to those who by patient continuance in doing good seek for glory, honor, and immortality.

Change the WAY YOU THINK! If you keep trying to improve your life as an orphan does-- posturing yourself as a victim and manipulating others for selfish and short-term gain-- you will lose in the end.

But if you SUBMIT to God, BELIEVE in Jesus, and start TALKING and ACTING as a son or daughter, then you'll win. What does that mean? How do I talk and act like a child of God?

You seek glory, honor, and immortality.

Believers long for GLORY. You should desire to walk in the same level of peace, love, joy, anointing, power, hope, faith, and influence that Jesus did.

To follow Jesus is to want HONOR. You should long to be known in heaven and hell, to walk with authority, to be famous for empowering others, and for leaving a legacy for your grandchildren.

Disciples hope for IMMORTALITY. You must hunger to LIVE FOREVER in the presence of God, making an eternal impact, and receiving the reward for your labor.

Not only should you want those things, but **you should SEEK them every day,** patiently adding value to more and more people. Glory, honor, and immortality make the game of life meaningful and exciting.

Whoever adds the most value to the most people using the tools Jesus provides wins!

Are you bored with everyday life? How can you seek glory, honor, and immortality today?

_____

_____

_____

_____

_____

_____

_____

_____

_____

_____

_____

_____

_____

_____

_____

_____

_____

_____

_____

_____

_____

_____

_____

DAY 31: Romans 4-7

I Reckon

Likewise you also, reckon yourselves to be dead indeed to sin, but alive to God in Christ Jesus our Lord.

It doesn't matter that Jesus died.

It makes no difference that He conquered sin and death, rising from the grave on the third day.

It's worthless that Jesus ascended into heaven and poured out the Holy Spirit, connecting heaven and earth.

All of the freedom, acceptance, power, love, and revelation that He procured does you no good.

UNLESS...

You change the way you think about yourself.

You see, Jesus did all the heavy lifting, setting the legal precedent for your freedom, and providing the grace for you to become **awesome**.

But unless you change the way you think about yourself, you won't benefit from Jesus' work at all.

Paul said to **RECKON yourself dead to sin and alive to God.** That means you must **BELIEVE what Jesus did already worked, CONSIDER yourself a new person, and live as if you're amazing.**

Jim Rhon said it best in one of my favorite quotes: **"If I will change, everything will change for me."**

What can you PRACTICE thinking about yourself today that will enable you to experience the quality of life Jesus desires for you?

_____

_____

_____

_____

_____

_____

_____

_____

_____

_____

_____

_____

_____

_____

_____

_____

_____

_____

_____

_____

DAY 32: Romans 8-11

The Things Of The Spirit

For those who live according to the flesh set their minds on the things of the flesh, but those who live according to the Spirit, the things of the Spirit.

Paul said to set your mind on the things of the Spirit, not the things of the flesh. **What do you think he meant?** Every human being is designed by God to need clean water and nutritious food, exercise, adequate sleep, clothing and shelter, love and affection, a sense of belonging, meaningful work, sexual fulfillment, and stories that fascinate us. None of those things are evil-- God created us with those requirements built into our DNA.

You cannot repent for wanting to satisfy those cravings, and they will never go away. However, it is the way we get those things that makes all the difference in the world.

You see, there are only two ways to approach life-- **you are either a son or an orphan.** It was paramount that the SON of God came to reconnect us with the FATHER because only a SON can make us sons. No other religion or way of thinking can reconcile us with the Father.

As long as you FEEL like an orphan, you will set your mind on survival. You will try to fulfill your basic human needs the best you know how. **But when you are a son or daughter, you allow the Father take responsibility for your needs, and you set your mind on the things of the Spirit.** You spend your time thinking about what the Spirit is saying and doing, glorifying Jesus, and adding value to people.

Jesus wants you to stop wasting your creativity on food and clothes and seek first the Kingdom of God, and as a result, the Father will take care of your needs.

Do you practice meditation, journalling, getting out in nature, gathering for worship, and other habits that help you set your mind on the things of the Spirit? How can you practice them more?

_____

_____

_____

_____

_____

_____

_____

_____

_____

_____

_____

_____

_____

_____

_____

_____

_____

_____

_____

_____

_____

_____

_____

DAY 33: Romans 12-15

The Renewed Mind

And do not be conformed to this world, but be transformed by the renewing of your mind, that you may prove what is that good and acceptable and perfect will of God.

What determines your ability to impact the people around you?

Is it fate? Are you waiting on God's timing? Perhaps it is your gift mix? Maybe it is the environment or the people that surround you? Could it be talent, resources, or divine favor?

I don't think so.

Jesus demonstrated the perfect will of God: people reconnecting with the Father, feeling a sense of belonging, getting healthy and free, and becoming powerful builders of the Kingdom of God on the earth.

So what determines if you can prove the will of God as Jesus did?

The way you think.

Is the world supposed to get better or worse? Is God a loving Father or a cruel taskmaster? Are you supposed to touch thousands of lives or survive to the end? Do you divide your life between secular and sacred, or are you always building the kingdom? Do your words carry authority?

Are you willing to sell, lead, go on camera, and deliver results for others, or are you just paying bills and entertaining yourself?

THE WAY YOU THINK ABOUT YOURSELF IS THE DETERMINING FACTOR WHETHER YOU IMPACT THE WORLD OR STRUGGLE TO SURVIVE.

The RENEWING of your mind should be your number one focus.
How can you make it more of a priority today?

_____

_____

_____

_____

_____

_____

_____

_____

_____

_____

_____

_____

_____

_____

_____

_____

_____

_____

_____

_____

DAY 34: Romans 16 - 1 Corinthians 3

Abundant Hope

Now may the God of hope fill you with all joy and peace in believing, that you may abound in hope by the power of the Holy Spirit.

Do you know where joy and peace come from? BELIEVING.

Rest and happiness form inside you when your mind, emotions, speech, and actions are all aligned in pursuit of something you believe is God's will.

You FEEL great when you want the same things for yourself as God does, and HOPE abounds in your heart.

However, we usually do the opposite. We don't want to get our expectations too high because we're afraid of disappointment.

The way we talk, feel, act, and think doesn't agree with God's desires for us, and we're scared to go after stuff because we're afraid to fail.

Therefore, we live without **believing,** and we miss out on the peace, joy, and hope that comes with it.

For some reason, we think that God is going to wave His magic wand and drop something awesome in our lap, and then we'll be happy.

But it doesn't work that way. **It's BELIEVING that makes you happy, not the fulfillment.**

It's the passionate pursuit of the dreams God put in your heart that make life worth living, not sitting on "someday" beach waiting for the perfect guy/girl/job/home/trip/opportunity to drop in your lap.

It's NOT the changing of our outer CIRCUMSTANCES that makes us happy, but rather our internal TRANSFORMATION. How are you hoping to become more like Jesus today?

_____

_____

_____

_____

_____

_____

_____

_____

_____

_____

_____

_____

_____

_____

_____

_____

_____

_____

_____

_____

DAY 35: 1 Corinthians 4-7

All Things Are Yours

For all things are yours: whether Paul or Apollos or Cephas, or the world or life or death, or things present or things to come--all are yours.

Do you realize your level of ACCESS?

You didn't sign up for a cult when you began following Jesus, nor did you join a religious organization. This is not a self-help group or a ten-step program to cope with your problems. You are not jumping on the bandwagon of the latest guru to improve your life by two percent.

When you follow Jesus, you become a son or daughter of THE CREATOR. **His Spirit came to live in you, giving you ACCESS to EVERYTHING.** You have the login and password to the mind of God, and the manual to teach you how to search.

All things are yours.

Others can't understand what is going on in you because they still think like orphans.

Faith, hope, love, gratitude, forgiveness, worship, and community are not random suggestions to improve your life-- **they are the ACCESS portals** through which you receive the revelation and power to change the world.

Changing the way you think, feel, talk, and act are not religious duties earning you points so you can be rewarded in the sweet by and by.

You are the light of the world, the hope of the nations. Identifying yourself as a child of God and aligning your mind, emotions, actions, and words with His is the way you make the world look like heaven.

What does God think about you that you have trouble believing? How can you practice thinking differently today?

_____

_____

_____

_____

_____

_____

_____

_____

_____

_____

_____

_____

_____

_____

_____

_____

_____

_____

_____

DAY 36: 1 Corinthians 8-11

Run To Win

Do you not know that those who run in a race all run, but one receives the prize? Run in such a way that you may obtain it.

Run to win. It sounds simple, but it's hard to execute sometimes.

Think about the areas of your life: family, friends, work, ministry, health, money. **Are you pursuing excellence in each one?**

Are you living in such a way that you become the best in the world at what you do? Why not?

There are plenty of reasons not to-- fear of failure, insecurity, emotional trauma, and stress from an overcrowded life.

But really-- why not?

You don't think of yourself as a winner.

You believed the lie that your thoughts, feelings, actions, skills, speech, habits, and relationships are outside of your control.

In short, **you feel like a victim in some area of your life**. You don't think you can win, or you believe it wouldn't make a difference if you did.

BUT IT'S NOT TRUE!

Every aspect of your **inner life** is under your control, and you have access to the Spirit of the Living God.

RUN TO WIN.

What could you be great at? What are you going to do to get there?

_____

_____

_____

_____

_____

_____

_____

_____

_____

_____

_____

_____

_____

_____

_____

_____

_____

_____

_____

_____

_____

DAY 37: 1 Corinthians 12-15

What Is Jesus Doing?

Imitate me, just as I also imitate Christ.

What would Jesus do? That question became popular several years ago as a way to settle a moral dilemma. If faced with two options, ask, "What would Jesus do?" and then make your decision based on what you think He would do if He were in your situation.

It's not a terrible way to make choices, I guess, but it's not what Paul taught the Corinthians. He said, "Imitate me, just as I also imitate Christ." Paul was not making moral decisions based on Jesus' track record-- **he was in a relationship with the living Christ.**

He was not asking, "What would Jesus do?" **He talked to Jesus, who was alive and well, and asked Him, "What are you doing?"** Paul knew that he was Jesus' hands and mouth on the earth, and he wanted to live in perfect alignment with what Jesus was currently doing.

There are only two options for the believer. Either you are a world-changer receiving orders from heaven, or you are following a world-changer and learning from them. (You can be both, by the way.) There are no survivors or spectators in the kingdom-- **there are only world-changers and interns.**

If you don't fit into one of those two categories, or you feel like a victim in some area of your life, CHANGE THE WAY YOU THINK.

Find a world-changer and start modeling what they do. Adjust your environment-- change who you listen to, what you read and watch, where you go, who you hang out with, etc.-- and your feelings will align with what Jesus is doing right now.

What is Jesus doing in your area, and how can you participate?

_____

_____

_____

_____

_____

_____

_____

_____

_____

_____

_____

_____

_____

_____

_____

_____

_____

_____

_____

_____

_____

DAY 38: 1 Corinthians 16 - 2 Corinthians 3

What Are Your Assumptions?

For I delivered to you first of all that which I also received: that Christ died for our sins according to the Scriptures.

The way you see the world, yourself, and God is the most important thing in life. Your perspective touches everything, influencing how you think, feel, and act, and ultimately, the results you get. **If you start with the wrong assumptions, you will end up in the wrong place.**

Here are seven key assumptions that every believer must embrace if they want to follow Jesus and impact the world:

THE WORLD IS SUPPOSED TO GET BETTER, NOT WORSE. If you believe that it's all going to fall apart in the end, you can't do the work necessary to make the world a better place.
THERE IS NO SUCH THING AS SACRED AND SECULAR.
Everything we do should honor God and add value to people, including our work, rest, and entertainment.
YOUR HEART IS GOOD. What Jesus did for you worked; all that's left is to believe it.
YOU ARE NOT A VICTIM. I don't care what you went through; Jesus didn't get up from the grave so you could feel sorry for yourself.
YOU ARE NOT WAITING ON GOD. There is waiting in life-- between sowing and reaping-- but God already did everything necessary for you to prosper.
YOU ARE A WORLD-CHANGER. There are no survivors or spectators in the Kingdom, only world-changers and interns.
YOU ARE JUST ONE IDEA AWAY. If you believe the other six assumptions, and you cultivate your heart into fertile soil, **all it takes is one idea from God to turn any area of your life into a fruitful field.**

Are you in alignment with each of the seven assumptions? Why or why not?

_____

_____

_____

_____

_____

_____

_____

_____

_____

_____

_____

_____

_____

_____

_____

_____

_____

_____

_____

DAY 39: 2 Corinthians 4-7

Self-Imposed Restrictions

You are not restricted by us, but you are restricted by your own affections.

Be honest with yourself-- there is no one holding you back. It's not your parents, pastor, boss, ex-husband, or group of friends-- **you just don't want to.** You could lose the weight, write the book, make some extra money, deepen that relationship, or whatever, but the desire to do so is not as strong as the pain associated with the changes you would need to make. **So you settle into survival mode, wishing for better results without changing your behavior.** So here's the all-important QUESTION-- if desire is the ONLY way to be successful, **how do I make myself want something?** Now that's a good question, and I have an answer for you.

First, change your IDENTITY. Change the way you think about yourself by dwelling on God's purpose for your life as seen in the Bible, your prophetic words, testimonies of how God has used you, and desires He put in your heart. TALK YOURSELF INTO BECOMING WHO GOD CREATED YOU TO BE.

Next, consider the PEOPLE who would benefit from the changes you need to make. Think about all of the people you care about (including yourself), and how their life would improve if you changed. LOVE IS THE BEST MOTIVATOR BY FAR, SO USE IT TO HELP YOU DO HARD THINGS.

Finally, change your ENVIRONMENT. Change what you watch, what you listen to, who you hang out with, where you go, what you read, and how you spend your time, and your feelings will begin to align with your new environment. YOU CAN CREATE DESIRE BY LISTENING TO STORIES THAT INSPIRE YOU.

Are you restricting your life with underdeveloped desires? What stories can you connect with emotionally to change that?

_____

_____

_____

_____

_____

_____

_____

_____

_____

_____

_____

_____

_____

_____

_____

_____

_____

_____

_____

DAY 40: 2 Corinthians 8-11

Follow Through

Now you also must complete the doing of it; that as there was a readiness to desire it, so there also may be a completion out of what you have.

You said you wanted to do it. **Halfway through the how-to book you bought, something came up, and you never got back to it.** Your intentions are good. Even after all this time, the desire is still there.

BUT YOU HAVEN'T DONE IT.

Like the Corinthians, you set out a year ago to finish that project that would transform your life and add value to a bunch of people, but there it sits, gathering dust.

Are you waiting for permission? Is fear holding you back?

I understand how overwhelmed you feel when you think about all that needs doing and how little time there is to do it. Whatever the reason you haven't done it yet, it's not too late.

DO IT TODAY!

Don't wait until tomorrow. Forget your crazy schedule this week and do it right now. Make the call, pay for the service, set up the account, write the check, set up the meeting, or whatever you need to do.

Fear doesn't tell you what to do anymore.

You're not the same person you were a year ago.

You have permission to BE AWESOME today. Just do it.

What can you do today to move you a little closer to the life you want?
Do it...

_____

_____

_____

_____

_____

_____

_____

_____

_____

_____

_____

_____

_____

_____

_____

_____

_____

_____

_____

DAY 41: 2 Corinthians 12 - Galatians 2

Living Without Anxiety

Become complete. Be of good comfort, be of one mind, live in peace; and the God of love and peace will be with you.

Become complete, be single-minded, and live at peace. That's the advice Paul gave the Corinthians, and wow, could we benefit from it today. **But how?**

How do we live without anxiety? I'm not going to pretend to have all the answers, but I have found one thing that makes a big difference-- COMMITMENT.

It's not trying circumstances that cause stress-- **it's a divided heart.** When we're unsure of how we feel, what we think, or what to do we get anxious.

So here's a simple trick that helps a ton-- **make a short-term commitment.** Let's say I don't know whether to go through door number one or door number two, and I keep going back and forth on the pros and cons of each. **The longer I linger in indecision, the more stressed out I get**.

The best way to live at peace is to go all-in on one of them for a limited time (a week, month, or year, etc.) You're not deciding what to do forever. Make a commitment to do something for a limited time with all of your might, and then reevaluate.

The same process works for your thoughts and feelings as well. If you're not sure what you believe about something, pick a side and go deep for a while. Don't allow yourself to argue until you have spent the allotted time all-in. **It works-- try it.**

Are you feeling anxious because of a divided heart? What commitment can you make to become complete? How long will you commit?

_____

_____

_____

_____

_____

_____

_____

_____

_____

_____

_____

_____

_____

_____

_____

_____

_____

_____

_____

DAY 42: Galatians 3-6

Why Not You?

God shows personal favoritism to no man-- for those who seemed to be something added nothing to me.

God shows personal favoritism to no one. Period.

That means all those people out there changing the world have no more favor than you do.

World-changers are not special, nor were they born with unusual talent. They're just like you.

So why are they making a significant impact, and you're not? Three reasons:

They think of themselves the same way God thinks about them.

They develop emotional wholeness internally and in their relationships with others.

They leverage time and money for maximum impact.

It's not our circumstances or some magic fairy dust that distinguishes between those "favored" by God and us ordinary folks-- **it's just faith, hope, and love.**

How you think about yourself will determine your impact on the world.

So why not you? Why can't you change the world? You can, and you should. **Nothing is standing between you and a fruitful life except you.**

Have you let yourself believe that other people have more favor than you, and that's why their life is better? How can you root out that victim mentality and go after your dreams?

_____

_____

_____

_____

_____

_____

_____

_____

_____

_____

_____

_____

_____

_____

_____

_____

_____

_____

_____

DAY 43: Ephesians 1-4

What Do You Pray For?

That the God of our Lord Jesus Christ, the Father of glory, may give to you the spirit of wisdom and revelation in the knowledge of Him.

Have you ever studied the prayers in the Bible? It's fascinating what the Holy Spirit prompted guys like Paul to pray because it gives us insight into what we need the most.

The prayers we often hear (or pray) sound something like this, "God, heal so and so," or "Father, I need money for that thing," or "Why did this happen to me?" But that's not the kind of prayers modeled or taught in the Bible.

In Ephesians 1, Paul writes to a group of believers he has never met, letting them know what he is praying for them. **Do you know what the ONLY request he makes for them, the thing that would push the domino over leading to an abundant life?**

REVELATION.

Paul prays that they would understand WHO THEY ARE and WHAT THEY ALREADY HAVE ACCESS TO. **He knows that if the Ephesians get that, they get everything.** The same is true for you and me. **When we THINK correctly about ourselves, the entire kingdom opens up to us.** Jesus already took care of the legal stuff for us to be AWESOME, but we can only access what we BELIEVE.

When you pray, switch your focus from asking for the thing you want (which implies you have no authority) to requesting more UNDERSTANDING about who you are and the power already at work in you.

Do you pray for yourself? What do you ask for? Quit making victim requests, expecting God to do your work for you. Pray for more REVELATION about what you already possess.

_____

_____

_____

_____

_____

_____

_____

_____

_____

_____

_____

_____

_____

_____

_____

_____

_____

_____

_____

_____

DAY 44: Ephesians 5 - Philippians 2

Walk Worthy

I, therefore, the prisoner of the Lord, beseech you to walk worthy of the calling with which you were called.

Can I be real with you? The old religious model where there is one "minister" for every hundred believers is, well, stupid. Did Jesus rise from the grave and pour out the Holy Spirit so a bunch of victims could gather to receive "ministry" every week?

Are we supposed to spend all week at jobs we don't like, stressed out about money, destroying our health, arguing with our family, and then medicating the pain with all sorts of nonsense? Is this what Jesus had in mind, a group of unhealthy, broken victims going to the hospital (I mean church) now and then to get treatment? **I think not.**

As Paul explains in Ephesians, every believer has a calling. We are all kings and priests with a special grace from Jesus to build each other up and make the world a better place. **It irks me to see the light of the world, the people who are the answer to every problem on earth, hiding in a corner trying to hang on until someone comes to rescue them from this "awful" world.**

This is our planet. We are sons and daughters of God, ruling with Him to break the back of orphan thinking and bring His peace to society.

There are no orphans, victims, beggars, or survivors in the kingdom. You are either a world-changer or an intern; those are the only options.

We all heal the sick, hear from God, worship with abandon, and use the grace Jesus gave us to add value to others.

What areas of your life are being influenced by a victim mentality?
What are you going to do about it?

_____

_____

_____

_____

_____

_____

_____

_____

_____

_____

_____

_____

_____

_____

_____

_____

_____

_____

_____

_____

_____

DAY 45: Philippians 3 - Colossians 2

Think Like Jesus

Let this mind be in you which was also in Christ Jesus.

How did Jesus think about Himself?

Was He anxious, insecure, or fearful?

Of course not.

Was He prideful and arrogant, bullying His way to the front of the line?

No way.

Orphans must choose between playing the victim to manipulate people into giving them what they want and bullying others to take it. Sons and daughters don't have to play that game.

Because we are already safe, loved, secure, accepted, and provided for, we can rest.

The Father's purpose for Jesus was to make Him so famous that everyone in the world would know His name and submit to His leadership. You can't get any bigger than that.

However, the Father's plan to make Jesus famous involved humility, service, and sacrificing His life.

Jesus said yes to both. He SUBMITTED to being great and serving His way to the top.

So how does Jesus think? **He thinks like a Son-- and so should you.**

How does Jesus think about himself different than you think about yourself?

_____

_____

_____

_____

_____

_____

_____

_____

_____

_____

_____

_____

_____

_____

_____

_____

_____

_____

_____

DAY 46: Colossians 3 - 1 Thessalonians 2

Set Your Mind

Set your mind on things above, not on things on the earth.

God designed you to be free and exercise authority in every area of your life. He doesn't want to control you; in fact, He refuses to.

Jesus came to reconnect you to the Father, but you don't get the benefits of what He did unless you agree with Him. Therefore, **the way you think is the most important thing in the world.**

When you set your mind on who God says you are, what Jesus did for you, what the Holy Spirit is saying and doing, and how you can partner with Him to add value to others, you create a productive ecosystem in your soul.

Your awareness fosters greater agreement which gives you increased access to heaven. Instead of drawing from your own resources, you get access to God's love, grace, power, revelation, and wealth.

You were never meant to live disconnected from the Father, drifting through life on your own.

You were designed to stay connected, and it's your THOUGHT LIFE that builds the bridge.

You don't have to fill your day with office gossip, cat videos, and negative news reports. You're not required to worry about money and wallow in loneliness.

You control what you think about, so set your mind on the things that set you up to succeed.

The way you think is the most important thing in the world. How can you set your mind on things above today?

_____

_____

_____

_____

_____

_____

_____

_____

_____

_____

_____

_____

_____

_____

_____

_____

_____

_____

_____

_____

_____

_____

DAY 47: 1 Thessalonians 3 - 2 Thessalonians 1

Growing In Love

But we urge you, brethren, that you increase more and more.

What does love look like? More specifically, **how do you show someone who doesn't feel loved that you care about them?**

I'm sure there are many ways, but I want to highlight one.

You listen to them.

You take the time to hear what is going on in their lives, how they feel, and why they feel that way.

It's not complicated, but it can be hard to do.

Often, when people are hurt or struggling, they lash out in some way.

If you can get past your initial reaction to put your guard up and hear what they are trying to say, then you're doing better than most.

But many times it's hard for them to understand or explain what they're feeling, so you must exercise patience and compassion and help them discover why they're hurt.

Be careful not to try to fix everything or give premature advice, but instead ask simple questions covered with grace.

Lead them to a place of greater awareness while making then feel safe.

Nothing communicates love like a genuine, patient ear ready to hear what is on their heart.

How can you grow in love today? Who can you listen to with greater compassion?

_____

_____

_____

_____

_____

_____

_____

_____

_____

_____

_____

_____

_____

_____

_____

_____

_____

_____

_____

_____

DAY 48: 2 Thessalonians 2 - 1 Timothy 2

Fight For Your Future

This charge I commit to you, son Timothy, according to the prophecies previously made concerning you, that by them you may wage the good warfare.

You are not an accident. You are here for a reason, and the world needs you at your best. Many of us, however, are passive when it comes to walking out our identity and purpose. We have a vague idea of who God called us to be, but **we sit around waiting on God instead of pursuing our passion.**

There are three fundamental ways to know what your purpose is: **prophecies, testimonies, and desires.**

God talks to us through mental impressions, dreams, Scripture verses, unusual circumstances, songs, sermons, and prophecies from others to leave clues about who we are. Pay attention to what He says and take it seriously.

Also, watch for patterns of how God uses you to add value to others-- those testimonies are an indicator of your identity.

Finally, don't discount your desires. The longings inside you were placed there by God to drive you into your purpose.

Take the time to get clear about your future, but don't stop there. **Merely knowing why you were born doesn't make it happen, you have to FIGHT for it.**

Use the prophecies, testimonies, and desires to launch an all-out war on survival and complacency, and do whatever it takes to fulfill your role on the earth.

Why are you here? What direction do your prophecies, testimonies, and desires point you in? How can you fight to fulfill your destiny?

_____

_____

_____

_____

_____

_____

_____

_____

_____

_____

_____

_____

_____

_____

_____

_____

_____

_____

_____

_____

DAY 49: 1 Timothy 3-6

Go All In

Meditate on these things; give yourself entirely to them, that your progress may be evident to all.

Do you know what will change the world (and make me smile until my face hurts)?

The world will change **when you know how God thinks about you.** Pretty simple, right?

Oh, there's one more thing. **You must think about yourself the same way-- you can't disagree with Him.**

When you know how God feels about you and why you were born, and you live in full agreement with it-- look out!

My dream is for you to understand your IDENTITY and pursue it with passion. Nothing else would make me, God, or you happier, or have a more significant effect on the planet.

Except for one thing-- **you making money doing what you're called to do.** Now that would be AMAZING!

Imagine it (come on, just let yourself imagine for a second.) **What if you were crystal clear about your identity and purpose, and you made your living doing the thing God called you to do.**

You could FOCUS on the thing that makes you smile AND add tons of value to others AND master your craft AND care for your family at the same time. **Go for it.**

What could you do for a living that would bring deep satisfaction and make the world a better place? What's your plan to get there?

_____

_____

_____

_____

_____

_____

_____

_____

_____

_____

_____

_____

_____

_____

_____

_____

_____

_____

_____

_____

DAY 50: 2 Timothy 1-4

7 Stages Of A Fruitful Life

For God has not given us a spirit of fear, but of power and of love and of a sound mind.

There are seven stages we go through if we are to live a fruitful life. Remember, in this analogy, **your heart is the soil, the seeds are ideas God gives you, and the fruit is the results you produce to help others.**

1. BUY IN. It's time to get rid of shame and blame, take responsibility for your heart, and believe that you are supposed to live a fruitful life. Unless you take OWNERSHIP of your thoughts, feelings, words, and actions and say no to a victim mentality, you will never get past this stage.

2. SOIL PREP. Once you're ALL-IN, it's time for personal growth. You immerse yourself in learning, doing everything you can to master your health, relationships, time, money, thought life, emotions, and confidence.

3. CONTRIBUTION. Now your heart is fertile, and you start trying to help others any way you can. You grow a little of everything, paying attention to what produces the most fruit, adds the most value, people are willing to pay for, is sustainable, and you enjoy.

4. PRODUCT CREATION. This stage is all about narrowing your focus. You find out what is working and do more of it. Along the way, you eliminate the things that don't produce the results you want and master the things that do.

5. PLATFORM BUILDING. Now that you have a way to add value, you begin expanding your distribution. You take your fruit to the market and gather a group of raving fans.

6. SCALE. Once things are working, you build a team and use technology to multiply your effectiveness.

7. IMPACT. At this stage, you fine-tune everything to see how you can add the most value to the most people.

Have you taken full responsibility for your life? What stage are you in? What is your plan to get to the next stage?

_____

_____

_____

_____

_____

_____

_____

_____

_____

_____

_____

_____

_____

_____

_____

_____

_____

_____

_____

DAY 51: Titus 1 - Philemon

Preach The Word!

Preach the word! Be ready in season and out of season. Convince, rebuke, exhort, with all longsuffering and teaching.

When most people think about preaching, they picture an old white guy standing behind a pulpit explaining a Bible verse to a congregation. I want to expand your understanding of the concept.

The message of the kingdom is simple: Jesus, the Son of God, came to earth to empower all of us to **stop living like orphans.** He reconnected us with the Father, and together we make the world a better place.

Preaching is marketing, plain and simple. It's telling stories to persuade someone to stop living like an orphan and a victim, believe in Jesus, and start thinking like a son or daughter of God.

We preach to help others adopt a new IDENTITY. Once they have done that, then and only then can they learn how to do life better.

So, whether you are a singer or musician, health and fitness professional, writer and speaker, business owner, government official, or just a parent or grandparent, the job is the same-- **preach the word.**

Help others think like sons and daughters, and then after they have bought in and are listening to you, teach them how to live like one.

We are not in the business of using shame to manipulate people into following a list of rules. We market the best news in the world, **"You are not an accident. You are not alone. You are a son or daughter of the Creator, and together we add value to others and make the world look like heaven."**

How can you preach the Word today? What stories can you tell to help others adopt a new identity?

_____

_____

_____

_____

_____

_____

_____

_____

_____

_____

_____

_____

_____

_____

_____

_____

_____

_____

_____

Becoming Effective

That the sharing of your faith may become effective by the acknowledgment of every good thing which is in you in Christ Jesus.

There are four kinds of people in the world.

First, there are quitters. They are in such pain that they can't see a reason to go on. **Next, there are survivors.** These guys are hanging on, working hard, trying to keep up with their bills and maintain their relationships. **Third, there are achievers.** They figure out some of the principles of life and use them to their advantage, but they lack purpose. **Finally, there are world-changers.** This group know their God-given identity and purpose and have mastered the skills to distribute what they offer to others effectively.

Now, let's learn from the Apostle Paul the key to becoming effective. He says that if you want to share what you have with the world, **you must first acknowledge what God put inside you.** God dreamt about you in your mother's womb and fashioned you with a specific purpose. Shame, insecurity, blame, fear, anger, depression, and anxiety try to steal your identity away, but YOU DON'T HAVE TO LET THAT HAPPEN.

If you're struggling, try this exercise. Write down **something God said about you** (prophetic word, dream, scripture, etc.), **some way He used you before** to help others, and **a big desire** you have.

Now combine them in your mind to form a snapshot of the purpose God has for you. **Imagine yourself as the BEST IN THE WORLD at adding value to those people in that way, and then start living AS IF IT'S ALREADY TRUE.**

What has God put inside of you that the world needs? How can you become more effective sharing it?

_____

_____

_____

_____

_____

_____

_____

_____

_____

_____

_____

_____

_____

_____

_____

_____

_____

_____

_____

_____

DAY 53: Hebrews 5-8

Don't Get Sluggish

That you do not become sluggish, but imitate those who through faith and patience inherit the promises.

Have you ever heard the saying that the hardest part of doing anything is getting started? **The person who said that probably never finished anything, because that's nonsense.**

The most challenging part of doing anything worth doing is **right smack in the middle.**

When you start, you're excited. Ideas flow, and motivation surges in the beginning, but as time passes and the work gets tough, things begin to fall apart. Distractions and excuses fill up the empty part of your brain that used to contain all of those fantastic ideas you had at first.

Towards the end of a project, when you can see the finished line, motivation returns and pushes you onward. You look around, wondering where it came from and where it was from mile two until twenty-five of the marathon.

The first mile is exciting, and number twenty-six is rewarding, but **those twenty-four lonely miles in the middle are where you win the race.** If you're in the thick of it and are beginning to get sluggish, I feel you.

Don't quit. Split your goal up into manageable chunks and celebrate every mile marker you pass.

Remember who you are, the way you will feel when you cross the finish line, and the people who are counting on you, and KEEP MAKING PROGRESS.

Are you feeling sluggish in pursuit of your goals? How can you break them up into smaller parts and reinvigorate your enthusiasm?

_____

_____

_____

_____

_____

_____

_____

_____

_____

_____

_____

_____

_____

_____

_____

_____

_____

_____

_____

_____

_____

DAY 54: Hebrews 9-12

The Conscience

Let us draw near with a true heart in full assurance of faith, having our hearts sprinkled from an evil conscience and our bodies washed with pure water.

God designed you to be awesome.

The way your mind and heart interact with your body, others, and the spirit realm is incredible. Have you ever stopped to think about it?

Following Jesus has nothing to do with religion. An external set of rules to regulate behavior may be necessary for society, but that's not why Jesus came.

He came so you can THINK and FEEL like a son or daughter.

Before Christ, there was no way for your conscience to be clear; **it always felt like there was something wrong.**

Jesus made it possible for you to FEEL safe, confident, happy, secure, and clean. Through Him, you can walk down the street with full control of your mind and no sense of shame or guilt.

Believing in Jesus enables you to be like Him, fully integrating the natural and the supernatural. You can now look at anyone and genuinely want the best for them. You can hear from God, make demons leave, heal diseases, and forgive sins. Your body, work, creative expressions, and relationships are all GOOD.

If you live with guilt, shame, fear, or bitterness, you have believed a lie. Draw near to God with confidence, meditate on the truth of the gospel, and experience life with a clear conscience.

Is there any latent fear, anxiety, or shame restricting your forward progress? What lie is causing it?

_____

_____

_____

_____

_____

_____

_____

_____

_____

_____

_____

_____

_____

_____

_____

_____

_____

_____

_____

_____

DAY 55: Hebrews 13 - James 3

Doing The Word

But be doers of the word, and not hearers only, deceiving yourselves.

God has a purpose for your life, and **most likely, you already know what it is.** You may not be clear about all the details, but you got a general idea.

The Father drops hints in our dreams, stirs up our desires, prophesies through our friends, reveals secrets to our mentors, and uses our past testimonies to predict our future.

All of creation is begging for you to understand who you are and start living it out.

The question is not whether you've heard from God; it's WHAT ARE YOU DOING ABOUT IT?

James tells it to us straight-- if you want God's blessing, **you** must grow the ideas He gives you.

"Where do I start?" you say. It depends on where you're at right now.

Your life is like a garden. First, you prepare your heart by developing confidence, becoming emotionally whole, and learning to focus.

Then, you practice hearing from God, turning His ideas into desires, writing them down in detail, and planting them in your mind so they can grow.

Finally, you align your life with those desires by weeding out other things and watering what you want to bear fruit.

What can you start DOING today to grow the ideas God put in your heart and get better RESULTS?

_____

_____

_____

_____

_____

_____

_____

_____

_____

_____

_____

_____

_____

_____

_____

_____

_____

_____

_____

DAY 56: James 4 - 1 Peter 2

Changing Course

Look also at ships: although they are so large and are driven by fierce winds, they are turned by a very small rudder wherever the pilot desires.

So, you want to change your life.

You're tired of merely surviving-- you want to do something that matters.

Have you had enough of avoiding mirrors because you're disgusted by what you see, working a dead-end job that you can't stand, scrapping every month for barely enough to take care of your family, or feeling sorry for yourself one minute and then beating yourself up the next?

You want to be proud of yourself, to honor God with the gifts He gave you, and add real value to those around you.

You know it's going to take hard work and patience-- you're ready for that.

But where do you start?

How do you change the course of your life?

Just like a giant cruise ship changes direction with a tiny rudder, **you steer your life with your tongue.**

The way you talk to yourself, about yourself, and to others determines the direction you go.

So, you want to change your life? **Change the way you talk.**

How can you change the way you TALK to yourself, about yourself, and to God to change the course of your life?

_____

_____

_____

_____

_____

_____

_____

_____

_____

_____

_____

_____

_____

_____

_____

_____

_____

_____

_____

_____

_____

DAY 57: 1 Peter 3 - 2 Peter 1

Never Stop Growing

As newborn babes, desire the pure milk of the word, that you may grow thereby.

Did you know that the average person who listens to podcasts during the day makes three times as much as someone who listens to music? Interesting, isn't it? **Those who are hungry to learn out-produce those who are just passing the time three to one.**

Why do you think that is? Those eager to learn will end up more knowledgeable than others, but I think there's more to it than that.

I believe it has to do with identity (the way we think about ourselves.)

If you're a farmer producing crops to feed your community and provide for your family, then every detail matters. You need understanding about soil, weather, timing, markets, seeds, leadership, hiring, sales, and equipment.

But if you are a laborer picking tomatoes in a field getting paid by the hour, then all you care about is passing the time and trying to have fun while you work.

The shift from survivor to producer creates the hunger to learn and triples your fruitfulness.

Of course, the principle doesn't just apply to money. In every area of your life-- business, relationships, health, ministry, community-- **start thinking of yourself as a producer.** Stay hungry to learn, feeding on what God says about you and how you can add more value to others, and expect your results to grow along with your mind and heart.

*How can you PRACTICE thinking about yourself as a
PRODUCER today?*

_____

_____

_____

_____

_____

_____

_____

_____

_____

_____

_____

_____

_____

_____

_____

_____

_____

_____

_____

_____

_____

DAY 58: 2 Peter 2 - 1 John 2

Layers Of A Fruitful Life

For if these things are yours and abound, you will be neither barren nor unfruitful in the knowledge of our Lord Jesus Christ.

Fruitfulness is the ability to produce something that adds significant value to others. It is the process of receiving an idea from God, growing it, and distributing it in a way that impacts the world. Jesus said that the way we glorify the Father, and the entire point of the Christian life, is to **bear much fruit.**

So here's the question. **Why is it that one person can hear an idea and grow it into something that changes people's lives, while someone else gets the same idea and nothing happens?**

Those who remain unfruitful don't understand the process. We want to go straight from faith (our belief and confidence in God) to love (adding significant value to others), but we skip the steps in between.

Peter reminds us that believing in God is not enough to make you fruitful; there are layers in every fertile heart.

You start with **faith** (the way you think about God), but then you add **identity** (thinking of yourself the same way God thinks of you.) After identity, you add **knowledge** (the ideas you hear in your interaction with God.) From there you must develop **self-control** (the ability to motivate yourself.) Then you add **perseverance**, and after that, **integrity.** Next, you add **kindness** (your interpersonal communication skills), and then finally you get to **love.**

Remember, ideas are not enough-- you must be able to PRACTICE what you believe to grow and bear fruit. What layer can you add to your life today to improve your fruitfulness?

_____

_____

_____

_____

_____

_____

_____

_____

_____

_____

_____

_____

_____

_____

_____

_____

_____

_____

DAY 59: 1 John 3 - 2 John 1

Play To Win

For this purpose the Son of God was manifested, that He might destroy the works of the devil.

ME: I know this is a loaded question, but why did you come to the earth?
JESUS: Well, **I didn't come here to lose.** My Father sent Me to do a job, and I fulfilled His mandate perfectly.
ME: And what mandate was that?
JESUS: **To destroy the works of the devil.**
ME: Wow, that sounds aggressive. I thought you're the champion of meekness and humility?
JESUS: I am the KING of agreeing with My Father, changing the course of history, instituting the kingdom of God, restoring humanity, and leaving no doubt about who is in charge.
ME: I don't think I've ever seen this side of you. Are you always like this?
JESUS: I am full of compassion for those the devil has lied to, and I intend to lead them back to the Father. But **I don't play for second place.**
ME: This may be inappropriate, but **why do so many of your followers seem so, well, weak?**
JESUS: The enemy has tricked them into believing that they're still orphans, spreading lies to convince them to survive instead of thriving, but that's changing. **This is the greatest generation ever.**
ME: How so?
JESUS: **More people than ever before know that their voice matters, and together we are beating disease, loneliness, addiction, poverty, racism, and the victim mentality.**
ME: Thank you so much for your time. Any final thoughts?
JESUS: **PLAY TO WIN. Destroy the works of the devil in your own life, and then attack the problems I called you to solve.** We got this.

Are there any areas of your life where you're settling for second best?
What do you need to change to win?

_____

_____

_____

_____

_____

_____

_____

_____

_____

_____

_____

_____

_____

_____

_____

_____

_____

_____

_____

_____

DAY 60: 2 John 2 - Revelation 2

Prosper In All Things

Beloved, I pray that you may prosper in all things and be in health, just as your soul prospers.

God designed you to prosper in every area of your life. Your relationships, money, work, health, ministry, and hobbies should all be fruitful, adding value to your life and others.

Then why don't we? **What is holding us back?** We think that our prosperity is tied to a decision God makes, so we continue to plug along waiting on God to favor us. We associate fruitfulness with faithfulness, believing that if we keep showing up, God will notice. But that's not the way it works.

Athletes don't become world-class merely because they show up for practice every day, and laborers don't become wealthy because they're always on time.

The quality of our health, wealth, and relationships correlates directly to the prosperity of our souls. Our THOUGHTS, FEELINGS, and DESIRES must flourish before our life can. We must think about ourselves the way God does, learn to overcome negative emotions, find a coach, and practice what we believe before we can bear fruit.

You're not waiting on God, and you're not going to win the lottery. Faithfulness is not enough to produce fruit.

Align yourself with God's purpose, face your fears, believe the truth, do hard things, solve problems, and learn new skills. **The world inside you will eventually manifest in the world around you.**

Have you succumbed to the lottery mentality, waiting for God to bless you irregardless of the state of your soul? How can you change that?

_____

_____

_____

_____

_____

_____

_____

_____

_____

_____

_____

_____

_____

_____

_____

_____

_____

_____

_____

_____

_____

DAY 61: Revelation 3-6

Your New Name

I will give him a white stone, and on the stone a new name written which no one knows except him who receives it.

Your parents tried (well, most of them did.) They attempted to protect and raise you the best they knew how, but when you were born, they were still immature themselves.

Some of them abandoned, abused, or neglected you, leaving deep wounds. Others worked hard to give you what they never had growing up, setting you up to succeed.

But if we're honest (I'm speaking as a parent myself), **most of the time parents are just winging it,** doing the best they can with what they have.

The environment we grew up in and the names our parents gave us formed our identities, and they didn't always get it right.

But there's good news-- Jesus is offering you a **new name** based on the Father's purpose for your life.

The Father dreamed about you before you were born, contemplating the incredible impact you would have on the planet. Then life happened, piling heaps of garbage on your true identity and leaving you insecure and unaware of the Father's plan.

Listen as Jesus speaks to your heart right now, **"If you overcome, I'll tell you who you really are. It will be our secret; no one else needs to know. I know your heart-- I see you without the pile of garbage covering your identity and purpose. Allow Me the privilege of revealing it to you."**

How does the Father see you that is different from everyone else? How can you PRACTICE thinking about yourself that way?

_____

_____

_____

_____

_____

_____

_____

_____

_____

_____

_____

_____

_____

_____

_____

_____

_____

_____

_____

_____

DAY 62: Revelation 7-10

No Regrets

The Lamb who is in the midst of the throne will shepherd them and lead them to living fountains of waters. And God will wipe away every tear from their eyes.

Life hurts sometimes.

Accidents surprise us, slander irritates us, and betrayal smacks us in the face. Death, disease, and divorce gang up to push us into a ditch, and they'll keep us there if we let them.

But there is an answer, a way to experience real healing and happiness in this life and the next, and His name is Jesus.

He is the only way to go from feeling like an orphan to living as a son or daughter of the Creator, and He is the only way to emotional wholeness.

If you believe in Jesus and follow Him, one day you will rest in His love, free from all pain.

You are safe, forever.

There's only one thing you can't undo, a pain that will last longer than you intend and hurt more than any other-- regret.

DON'T LIVE WITH REGRET!

Do what you're called to do with all your might, take risks, and love people well. Forgive yourself for the mistakes you made and make the changes you need to make.

THIS IS YOUR OPPORTUNITY-- SEIZE IT!

How can you live TODAY so that you have no regrets? What do you need to let go of to move forward?

_____

_____

_____

_____

_____

_____

_____

_____

_____

_____

_____

_____

_____

_____

_____

_____

_____

_____

_____

_____

DAY 63: Revelation 11-14

He Shall Reign

The kingdoms of this world have become the kingdoms of our Lord and of His Christ, and He shall reign forever and ever!

Have you ever wondered, "who's in charge around here?" **Well, you are.**

Adam and Eve gave their dominion of the earth to the enemy when they voluntarily listened to and obeyed him. The result was a series of massive empires led by power-hungry dictators trying to take over the world. Satan ruled the world through fear, intimidation, greed, lust, hatred, and deception.

But Jesus put an end to his schemes, conquering death and taking back the leadership of the planet. Do you know what Jesus did with the authority He gained? **He gave it back to you.**

Since then, we the people have decided the fate of every generation.

Don't get me wrong, Jesus is still in charge-- but He doesn't rule like the enemy. **Manipulation is not His style.**

He empowers people and gives them the ideas, tools, and favor they need to succeed.

His political agenda includes every person on the planet voluntarily connecting with the Father, making their own decisions, and living happy, healthy, and productive lives.

The world will get better when you think about yourself the way God does, spend time with Jesus soaking up His ideas, and solve the problems He puts on your heart.

You're in charge of the planet-- it's your RESPONSIBILITY. *What are you going to do to make it better?*

_____

_____

_____

_____

_____

_____

_____

_____

_____

_____

_____

_____

_____

_____

_____

_____

_____

_____

_____

DAY 64: Revelation 15-18

The Next Jesus Movement

Then I looked, and behold, a Lamb standing on Mount Zion, and with Him one hundred and forty-four thousand.

Can I prophecy to you for a minute? I want to tell you about the next Jesus movement and the emerging generation of revivalists because I think you might be one of them.

God is calling a new breed of world-changers. Their core values are the same as every generation of believers. They believe the Bible, love worship embrace community, and practice the essential elements of the faith. **But the expression of their faith is radically different.** They are a band of CREATIVE ENTREPRENEURS who believe the world is supposed to get better, not worse. These passionate women and men are committed to solving the problems facing their generation.

This group couldn't care less about denominations, and they include every race, age, gender, and nationality. **Each of them MAKE MONEY doing what they're called to do, allowing them to master their craft.** They are artists, speakers, authors, tech specialists, singers, musicians, and coaches with a message to share and a tribe to gather.

Refusing to reserve spiritual gifts for church services, **they hear from God about business and relationships every day,** and they cooperate with the Holy Spirit at all times. They are confident in their IDENTITIES, emotionally whole, and AMBITIOUS. Not one of them is hiding in a corner waiting to be rescued, **choosing instead to develop themselves into the kind of person who makes an IMPACT.**

What do you think? Do you want to be a part of the next Jesus movement?

What is your role in the next Jesus movement?

_____

_____

_____

_____

_____

_____

_____

_____

_____

_____

_____

_____

_____

_____

_____

_____

_____

_____

_____

_____

_____

DAY 65: Revelation 19-22

He Who Overcomes

He who overcomes shall inherit all things, and I will be his God and he shall be My son.

Do you know what I want for you? **I want you to FEEL like a son or daughter of God.**

I want you to live without worry and experience the safety of being a part of a family. **I want you to be happy.**

I want you to find your identity and purpose, and walk it out with joy.

I want you to do meaningful work that adds value to people and makes the world a better place.

I want you to multiply your inheritance from your Father, and feel the bliss of God's presence.

I want you to hear from heaven and understand what to do with the ideas God gives you. **I want you to be proud of yourself.**

I want you to know the joy of treating others according to their possibilities, not their problems.

I want you to feel beautiful, appreciated, and loved.

I want you to relax, have fun, and enjoy your life.

You can experience all those things and more, but **you must OVERCOME** your insecurity, fear, doubt, worry, anger, and apathy. God will not do it for you; it's your responsibility. Will you overcome?

Will you TAKE RESPONSIBILITY for every thought, emotion, action, and result in your life? How?

_____

_____

_____

_____

_____

_____

_____

_____

_____

_____

_____

_____

_____

_____

_____

_____

_____

_____

_____

_____

_____

DAY 66

Five Years From Now

Five years from now, what will be the FRUIT of your life?

Based on the last few thousand years of recorded history, I can promise you a few things.

The government of your nation will be about the same as it is now.

Some of your friends will continue to encourage you, and some will keep whining and complaining.

Your family will be about like it is right now.

The laws, taxes, and economy will not be noticeably different.

Fall will come after summer, winter after fall, and then spring will follow winter.

God will be the same, as will the Bible.

You will continue to have good ideas, opportunities, and encounters with God. You will also experience difficulties and setbacks.

Everything will be almost exactly as it is now-- **EXCEPT YOU.**

For your life to change, you have to change. You must think better, feel happier, and want more.

Your fruitfulness does not depend on God, others, or your environment-- it's up to you.

*For your life to change, **you have to change**. God is already doing His part, and it's no one else's responsibility. What do you want the fruit of your life to be five years from now? Who do you need to become to get there?*

_____

_____

_____

_____

_____

_____

_____

_____

_____

_____

_____

_____

_____

_____

_____

_____

_____

_____

DAY 67

Identity & Intimacy

If you haven't noticed by now, **I want you to live a FRUITFUL life.** (And God does too!)

I want you to move **out of survival** (going around and around in the wilderness paying bills and putting out fires), **into a life of impact.**

Your life should produce more than what you need to exist-- **there should be something specific that you grow an abundance of that adds significant value to others.**

Your contribution could be a physical product, service, experience, message, or community-- I don't know. Whatever it is, it should draw people closer to the Father and improve their health, standard of living, or relationships.

Right now, you don't have to focus on the end results. All you need to do is cultivate the two variables that can increase your fruitfulness-- **identity and intimacy.**

To bear more fruit, you must either think about yourself better or spend more time with Jesus hearing what He has to say, or both. That's it.

Now you know what to focus on.

Develop your confidence, happiness, and focus, and then listen to Jesus more.

If you do those two things, you will live a fruitful life.

This book is designed to help you think about yourself like God does.
How will you continue to develop your identity after you finish the
10-Week Transformation? How do you plan to cultivate more intimacy
with Jesus?

_____

_____

_____

_____

_____

_____

_____

_____

_____

_____

_____

_____

_____

_____

_____

_____

_____

_____

_____

_____

_____

DAY 68

Consciousness

Your life is like a garden.

Your heart is the soil. **Your thoughts trigger emotions that lead to actions which produce results, or fruit.**

The container for this dynamic and beautiful ecosystem is called the SELF. Your self, or ego, or flesh, or whatever other names you may call it, is where the fruit of your life grows. It is not bad or good on its own; it is merely a reflection of how you care for it.

You are NOT the garden-- you are the GARDENER. You are a SPIRIT living in a body. You are not your thoughts; you are the THINKER of your thoughts.

Why does this matter? If you are the garden, meaning your thoughts DEFINE YOUR IDENTITY, then you can't change. If you think of yourself as an angry person because you had an angry thought, you can't do anything about it without having an identity crisis.

You are a spirit, who is a son of God, with dominion over your life, living in a kingdom of abundance-- THIS IS YOUR PRIMARY IDENTITY.

In your garden, you walk with God like Adam and Eve, communing with Him and receiving all the revelation and grace you need. You must become CONSCIOUS of yourself as a SPIRIT, DETACH from your flesh, and take full RESPONSIBILITY to cultivate your heart to change.

You're not the garden-- you're the gardener.

Consciousness is developed through the PRACTICE of meditation. When you set aside time away from distractions to WATCH YOURSELF THINK, you detach from your flesh so you can love yourself well. What is your plan to develop your identity as a spirit being? How do you plan to incorporate meditation into your day?

_____
_____
_____
_____
_____
_____
_____
_____
_____
_____
_____
_____
_____
_____
_____
_____
_____
_____

DAY 69

Love Yourself Well

Fruit grows in the soil of your heart. Ideas from heaven germinate in your thoughts, desires, and emotions and flourish through the water of God's grace.

A good and noble heart provides the PERFECT CONDITIONS for growth and results.

Right now, the garden of your heart may be the furthest thing from fruitful. Doubt from years of abuse and neglect may be poisoning your soul. Someone could have dumped a whole load of toxic garbage on you, leaving you to deal with the mess. Apathy and confusion may be draining your inner resources.

BUT NONE OF THAT MATTERS ANYMORE. **See yourself as a son, a spirit being made in the image of God tending the inheritance He gave you. Take responsibility for every thought, feeling, and action. Remove the worry from your mind and practice living in a world of abundance.**

You are the gardener, the one who watches and tends your SELF (your "self" is the body, mind, and emotions that your spirit lives in.) Therefore, you can LOVE YOURSELF WELL.

No matter what shape your garden is in right now, within a year you can start bearing fruit. All you need is the right care and attention.

IT'S NOT GOD'S JOB TO MAKE YOU FRUITFUL-- IT'S YOURS.

Love yourself well. Take the time to change the way you think and feel by PRACTICING what you believe.

How are you going to LOVE YOURSELF WELL?

_____

_____

_____

_____

_____

_____

_____

_____

_____

_____

_____

_____

_____

_____

_____

_____

_____

_____

_____

_____

_____

_____

DAY 70

What's Now?

You did it! You made it through the 10-Week Transformation! Now you know that it is your IDENTITY, or the way you think about yourself, that determines if you are fruitful or not.

Hopefully, you have begun some healthy habits that you can continue: meditation, going for a walk outside, eating lots of whole fruits and vegetables, getting enough sleep, journaling, and listening to the Bible. **But what do you do now?**

You need a project, a way to tell if what you're learning is working. You need something you can PRACTICE. May I make a suggestion? START WITH YOUR HEALTH.

Find a STORY of someone like you that went through a personal transformation and use it to create the belief that you can do the same. Use your WILLPOWER to change your IDENTITY-- don't start with your actions. Start eating more whole foods-- vegetables, fruits, legumes, nuts and seeds, and grains that don't need labels-- and PAY ATTENTION to how you feel.

When you want to eat junk-- processed or fast food-- ask yourself WHY? There will always be an EMOTIONAL reason you want to eat something that is not good for your long-term health. What is it? Don't allow yourself to use food to COMPENSATE for your "hard" life-- FIX YOUR LIFE INSTEAD.

Because you can **measure** if your health is getting better or worse by checking the scale, testing blood work, improving athletic performance, and evaluating how you feel, it's perfect for learning to love yourself well. Use the PRACTICE to become who you were created to be.

What is your plan to improve your health in the next 10 weeks? What STORY can you use to create belief? What thoughts, words, and feelings can you PRACTICE to change your identity around the subject of food?

_____

_____

_____

_____

_____

_____

_____

_____

_____

_____

_____

_____

_____

_____

_____

_____

Thank you for using the GOOD & NOBLE HEART
10-WEEK TRANSFORMATION to change the way you
think about yourself. I hope it was a valuable tool in your
personal development.

Ready to finally lose the extra weight and
transform your health once and for all? Go to
www.johnbradbury.co
to get FREE ACCESS to the online course
Why Can't I Lose Weight?
and begin your transformation today.

Made in the USA
Columbia, SC
15 May 2020

97343637R00090